THE PROSPERITY PARADIGM

Unlocking Wealth and Securing Financial Freedom

NANCY BARLOW

Copyright © 2024 by Nancy Barlow

TABLE OF CONTENT

INTRODUCTION 5

CHAPTER 1: THE FOUNDATION OF PROSPERITY... 9

 - Understanding the Psychology of Wealth 11

 - Cultivating a Prosperity Mindset..................... 15

 - Overcoming Limiting Beliefs and Financial Blocks 19

CHAPTER 2: STRATEGIC WEALTH BUILDING 24

 - The Power of Passive Income Streams........... 27

 - Investment Strategies for Long-Term Growth 32

 - Entrepreneurship: Building Assets and Creating Value 36

CHAPTER 3: FINANCIAL LITERACY AND MANAGEMENT... 42

 - Mastering the Basics of Budgeting and Saving 46

 - Debt Management and Elimination Strategies 51

- Maximizing Returns: Tips for Efficient Money Management.. 56

CHAPTER 4: LIFESTYLE DESIGN AND ABUNDANCE 63

- Defining Your Personal Vision of Prosperity. 67

- Cultivating a Lifestyle Aligned with Your Values 72

- The Art of Manifestation: Turning Dreams into Reality 77

CHAPTER 5: LEGACY, IMPACT, AND CONTRIBUTION.. 84

- Beyond Personal Wealth: Leveraging Prosperity for Good 88

- Creating a Lasting Legacy Through Generosity and Philanthropy 96

- Making a Meaningful Impact: Finding Purpose Beyond Profit 102

CONCLUSION... 110

INTRODUCTION

In an era where financial security is both a universal aspiration and a pressing concern for many, the pursuit of prosperity has become an essential endeavor. We live in a world abundant with opportunities, yet navigating the complexities of wealth accumulation and financial freedom often feels like traversing an intricate labyrinth. It's a journey marked by uncertainty, pitfalls, and occasional triumphs. In this landscape, understanding the underlying principles that govern prosperity becomes paramount.

Welcome to "The Prosperity Paradigm," a guidebook designed to illuminate the pathways to wealth, abundance, and lasting financial security. Within these pages, we embark on a transformative journey, redefining conventional notions of prosperity and unveiling the keys to unlock its full potential.

At its core, this book is a manifesto for the modern wealth seeker—an invitation to transcend mere accumulation and embrace a holistic vision of prosperity. Drawing upon insights from finance, psychology, entrepreneurship, and personal development, we delve deep into the foundations of wealth creation, uncovering timeless principles and practical strategies that stand as beacons of guidance in a sea of economic uncertainty.

But "The Prosperity Paradigm" is more than just a roadmap to financial success; it's a manifesto for personal empowerment. It challenges the status quo, urging readers to redefine their relationship with money, abundance, and success. By illuminating the intersections between mindset, behavior, and financial outcomes, it empowers individuals to cultivate a prosperity mindset—a mindset rooted in abundance, creativity, and purpose.

Throughout this book, we explore the fundamental pillars of the Prosperity Paradigm:

1. **Mindset Mastery:** Understanding the psychological underpinnings of wealth accumulation and cultivating a mindset primed for success.

2. **Strategic Wealth Building:** Navigating the intricacies of investments, entrepreneurship, and income generation to build sustainable wealth over time.

3. **Lifestyle Design:** Crafting a life of abundance and fulfillment that transcends material wealth, incorporating elements of purpose, passion, and contribution.

4. **Legacy and Impact:** Leveraging prosperity for the greater good, leaving a lasting legacy, and making a meaningful impact on the world.

As we embark on this journey together, it's important to recognize that prosperity is not merely a destination but a way of life—a continuous evolution fueled by intention, action, and growth. Whether you're a seasoned investor, an aspiring entrepreneur, or someone simply seeking greater financial security, "The Prosperity Paradigm" offers invaluable insights and practical tools to help you unlock your full potential and secure a future of abundance.

So, let us embark on this transformative odyssey—a journey that promises to redefine your relationship with wealth, unleash your innate potential, and ultimately, lead you to the pinnacle of prosperity.

CHAPTER 1: THE FOUNDATION OF PROSPERITY

In the pursuit of prosperity, one must first lay a solid foundation upon which to build. This foundation goes beyond mere financial knowledge or material wealth; it encompasses the very mindset and belief systems that shape our relationship with abundance. Welcome to Chapter 1: The Foundation of Prosperity.

At its core, prosperity is as much a state of mind as it is a measure of wealth. It begins with understanding the intricate interplay between psychology and economics—the subconscious beliefs and attitudes that govern our financial decisions and shape our outcomes. In this chapter, we delve deep into the underlying principles that form the bedrock of prosperity, exploring the nuances of mindset mastery and the art of cultivating a prosperous mindset.

But to truly unlock the doors to abundance, we must first confront and overcome the barriers that stand in our way. Throughout these pages, we confront the limiting beliefs and financial blocks that often sabotage our efforts towards wealth accumulation. By shining a light on these hidden obstacles, we empower ourselves to break free from their grip and pave a path towards financial freedom.

The journey towards prosperity is not just about accumulating wealth; it's about transforming our relationship with money and abundance on a fundamental level. It's about rewiring our subconscious programming, reframing our perceptions, and embracing a mindset primed for success. As we embark on this transformative odyssey, let us lay the groundwork for a future defined by abundance, fulfillment, and lasting prosperity.

- Understanding the Psychology of Wealth

The psychology of wealth is a multifaceted and complex subject that delves into the intricate interplay between our thoughts, emotions, beliefs, and behaviors surrounding money and abundance. Understanding the psychology of wealth is crucial for anyone seeking to achieve financial success and cultivate a mindset of prosperity. Here, we comprehensively discuss various aspects of the psychology of wealth:

1. **Belief Systems and Mindset:** Our beliefs about money and wealth are deeply ingrained and often shaped by our upbringing, culture, and experiences. These beliefs can either empower us or limit our potential for financial success. A scarcity mindset, for example, is characterized by beliefs that there is never enough money to go around, while an abundance mindset recognizes the infinite possibilities for wealth creation and abundance.

Cultivating a prosperity mindset involves identifying and challenging limiting beliefs and replacing them with empowering ones.

2. **Emotional Influences:** Our emotions play a significant role in our financial decisions and behaviors. Fear, greed, and impulse can lead to irrational decision-making, such as overspending, taking unnecessary risks, or avoiding investments altogether. Understanding and managing our emotions around money is essential for making sound financial choices and achieving long-term prosperity.

3. **Financial Self-Concept:** Our self-concept, or how we perceive ourselves about money and wealth, profoundly impacts our financial behaviors. Those with a strong sense of self-worth may be more inclined to pursue opportunities for wealth creation and financial independence, while those with low self-esteem may sabotage their success or feel unworthy of abundance. Developing a positive

financial self-concept involves building confidence, self-efficacy, and a sense of deservingness.

4. Behavioral Economics: Behavioral economics examines how cognitive biases and heuristics influence our economic decisions. Common biases such as loss aversion, anchoring, and herd mentality can lead to suboptimal financial outcomes. By understanding these biases, individuals can learn to recognize and mitigate their impact, making more rational and informed decisions.

5. Delayed Gratification and Impulse Control: The ability to delay gratification and exercise impulse control is a hallmark of financial success. Research has shown that individuals who can resist immediate rewards in favor of long-term goals tend to achieve greater wealth and success over time. Developing these skills involves strengthening self-discipline, setting clear goals, and practicing mindfulness.

6. Wealth and Happiness: The relationship between wealth and happiness is a complex one.

While financial security can contribute to overall well-being by reducing stress and providing opportunities for personal growth and fulfillment, the pursuit of wealth alone does not guarantee happiness. Studies have shown that beyond a certain threshold, increased wealth has diminishing returns on happiness. True prosperity encompasses not only financial success but also emotional well-being, fulfillment, and meaningful relationships.

In conclusion, the psychology of wealth is a vital area of study for anyone seeking to understand and optimize their relationship with money and abundance. By addressing beliefs, emotions, behaviors, and cognitive biases, individuals can cultivate a mindset of prosperity, make informed financial decisions, and ultimately achieve lasting wealth and fulfillment.

- Cultivating a Prosperity Mindset

Cultivating a prosperity mindset is about adopting a positive and empowering outlook on wealth, abundance, and success. It involves shifting one's beliefs, attitudes, and behaviors to align with the principles of prosperity and abundance. Here, we comprehensively discuss various aspects of cultivating a prosperity mindset:

1. **Awareness and Self-Reflection:** The first step in cultivating a prosperity mindset is becoming aware of one's current beliefs, attitudes, and behaviors surrounding money and abundance. This involves engaging in self-reflection and introspection to identify any limiting beliefs or negative thought patterns that may be holding you back from experiencing prosperity.

2. **Positive Affirmations and Visualization:** Positive affirmations and visualization techniques are powerful tools for reprogramming the

subconscious mind and reinforcing beliefs in abundance. By repeating affirmations such as "I am worthy of wealth and success" or "Money flows to me effortlessly," individuals can gradually shift their mindset towards prosperity. Visualization involves mentally rehearsing desired outcomes and experiencing the feelings of abundance as if they were already a reality.

3. **Gratitude Practice:** Cultivating a sense of gratitude is essential for fostering a prosperous mindset. Gratitude shifts the focus from scarcity to abundance by acknowledging and appreciating the blessings and abundance already present in one's life. Regularly practicing gratitude through journaling or daily reflections helps to cultivate a mindset of abundance and attract more positive experiences.

4. **Focus on Solutions, Not Problems:** A prosperity mindset is characterized by a solutions-oriented approach to challenges and setbacks. Instead of dwelling on obstacles or setbacks, individuals with

a prosperity mindset focus on finding creative solutions and opportunities for growth. They see challenges as temporary setbacks and view failures as valuable learning experiences on the path to success.

5. **Embrace Risk and Opportunity:** Cultivating a prosperity mindset involves embracing risk and seeing opportunities where others see obstacles. Instead of playing it safe and staying within their comfort zone, individuals with a prosperity mindset are willing to take calculated risks and step outside of their comfort zone in pursuit of their goals. They recognize that growth and success often require stepping into the unknown and embracing uncertainty.

6. **Surround Yourself with Positive Influences:** Surrounding yourself with positive influences and like-minded individuals who support your goals and aspirations is crucial for cultivating a prosperity mindset. This may involve seeking out mentors, joining mastermind groups, or surrounding yourself

with inspirational books, podcasts, and other resources that reinforce a mindset of abundance and success.

7. **Continuous Learning and Growth:** Cultivating a prosperity mindset is an ongoing process that requires continuous learning and personal growth. This involves investing in yourself through education, skill development, and personal development practices such as meditation, mindfulness, and self-care. By continuously expanding your knowledge and skills, you position yourself for greater opportunities and success in all areas of life.

In conclusion, cultivating a prosperity mindset is about adopting a positive and empowering outlook on wealth, abundance, and success. By becoming aware of limiting beliefs, practicing positive affirmations and gratitude, focusing on solutions, embracing risk and opportunity, surrounding yourself with positive influences, and committing to continuous learning and growth, you can cultivate a mindset of prosperity that attracts abundance and success into your life.

- Overcoming Limiting Beliefs and Financial Blocks

Overcoming limiting beliefs and financial blocks is a crucial step towards achieving prosperity and financial success. These beliefs are often deeply ingrained in our subconscious minds and can manifest as self-doubt, fear of failure, or feelings of unworthiness. Here, we comprehensively discuss various strategies for identifying and overcoming limiting beliefs and financial blocks:

1. **Awareness and Identification:** The first step in overcoming limiting beliefs is to become aware of them. This involves identifying the specific beliefs and thought patterns that are holding you back from achieving your financial goals. Common limiting beliefs include beliefs about money being scarce,

beliefs about one's worthiness or deservingness of wealth, and beliefs about the inevitability of failure.

2. **Challenge and Reframe:** Once you have identified your limiting beliefs, the next step is to challenge and reframe them. This involves questioning the validity of these beliefs and replacing them with more empowering and supportive beliefs. For example, if you believe that "money is the root of all evil," you might reframe this belief to "money is a tool that can be used for both good and bad, and I choose to use it for good."

3. **Visualization and Affirmations:** Visualization and affirmations can be powerful tools for reprogramming the subconscious mind and reinforcing positive beliefs. Visualization involves mentally rehearsing success scenarios and envisioning yourself achieving your financial goals. Affirmations are positive statements that you repeat to yourself regularly to affirm your desired outcomes and beliefs. By consistently practicing visualization and affirmations, you can gradually

overwrite limiting beliefs with more empowering ones.

4. Seeking Support: Overcoming limiting beliefs and financial blocks can be challenging, and it can be helpful to seek support from others. This may involve working with a coach, therapist, or mentor who can provide guidance, accountability, and encouragement as you work to overcome your limiting beliefs. Surrounding yourself with supportive friends and family members who believe in your potential can also be beneficial.

5. Taking Action: Taking action is a crucial step in overcoming limiting beliefs and financial blocks. Often, our fears and doubts dissipate once we take action towards our goals. Start by setting small, achievable goals that align with your financial aspirations, and take consistent steps towards achieving them. Celebrate your successes along the way, no matter how small, and use them as evidence to challenge your limiting beliefs.

6. **Embracing Failure as Learning:** Failure is a natural part of the journey towards success, and it's important to reframe failure as an opportunity for learning and growth rather than a reflection of your worth or abilities. When faced with setbacks or failures, reflect on the lessons learned and use them to inform your future actions. Remember that every successful person has faced failure along the way and that failure is not a permanent state but rather a stepping stone towards success.

7. **Practicing Self-Compassion:** Finally, it's important to practice self-compassion as you work to overcome limiting beliefs and financial blocks. Be gentle with yourself and recognize that changing deeply ingrained beliefs takes time and effort. Treat yourself with kindness and compassion, and celebrate your progress along the way, no matter how small.

In conclusion, overcoming limiting beliefs and financial blocks is a critical step towards achieving prosperity and financial success. By becoming aware of your limiting beliefs, challenging and reframing them, practicing visualization and affirmations, seeking support, taking action, embracing failure as learning, and practicing self-compassion, you can overcome the obstacles standing in your way and create a mindset of abundance and success.

CHAPTER 2: STRATEGIC WEALTH BUILDING

In the pursuit of financial freedom and abundance, strategic wealth-building serves as the cornerstone of long-term prosperity. It goes beyond mere accumulation of assets to encompass a deliberate and systematic approach to growing wealth over time. Welcome to Chapter 2: Strategic Wealth Building.

In this chapter, we embark on a journey to explore the multifaceted strategies and principles that underpin effective wealth accumulation. From prudent investment strategies to entrepreneurial endeavors, we delve into the myriad pathways that lead to lasting financial security and prosperity.

Strategic wealth building begins with a fundamental understanding of the principles of finance and economics. It involves making informed decisions about where and how to allocate resources to maximize returns and minimize risks. But beyond the technical aspects, strategic wealth building is also about cultivating a mindset of abundance and opportunity—a mindset that recognizes the potential for growth and prosperity in every circumstance.

Throughout this chapter, we will explore a variety of topics related to strategic wealth building, including:

1. **The Power of Passive Income Streams:** We examine the importance of generating passive income streams and explore various methods for creating sources of income that work for you even when you're not actively working.

2. **Investment Strategies for Long-Term Growth:** We delve into the world of investments, exploring different asset classes, investment vehicles, and strategies for building wealth over the long term while managing risks effectively.

3. **Entrepreneurship:** Building Assets and Creating Value: We discuss the role of entrepreneurship in wealth creation, highlighting the opportunities and challenges of starting and scaling a business, as well as the importance of creating value for customers and stakeholders.

4. **Financial Literacy and Management:** We emphasize the significance of financial literacy and effective money management skills in the wealth-building process, offering practical tips and strategies for budgeting, saving, and investing wisely.

5. **Maximizing Returns:** Tips for Efficient Money Management: We explore various techniques and tools for maximizing returns on investment, minimizing taxes, and optimizing financial resources to achieve your long-term financial goals.

By embracing the principles and strategies outlined in this chapter, you will be empowered to take control of your financial future and embark on a journey towards lasting prosperity and abundance.

Whether you're a seasoned investor, an aspiring entrepreneur, or someone simply seeking greater financial security, the insights and strategies presented here will provide invaluable guidance on your path to wealth and success. So, let us dive deep into the realm of strategic wealth-building and unlock the keys to financial freedom and prosperity.

- The Power of Passive Income Streams

The power of passive income streams lies in their ability to generate income with minimal ongoing effort or active involvement. Passive income streams can provide a steady source of revenue, allowing individuals to build wealth, achieve financial independence, and create the lifestyle of their dreams. Here, we comprehensively discuss various aspects of passive income streams and their significance in wealth creation:

1. **Definition and Types of Passive Income:**
Passive income is income generated from activities

in which an individual is not materially involved, such as rental income, dividends from stocks, interest from savings accounts, royalties from intellectual property, and affiliate marketing. There are various types of passive income streams, each with its benefits and considerations.

2. Benefits of Passive Income Streams:

- **Financial Freedom:** Passive income streams can provide financial stability and freedom by diversifying sources of income and reducing reliance on a single source of employment.

- **Flexibility:** Passive income allows individuals to have more flexibility in how they spend their time, as they are not tied to traditional 9-to-5 jobs.

- **Wealth Building:** Passive income streams have the potential to grow and compound over time, allowing individuals to build wealth and achieve their long-term financial goals.

- **Residual Income:** Passive income streams can continue to generate income even when individuals are not actively working, providing a source of residual income that can support them in retirement or during periods of illness or disability.

3. Creating Passive Income Streams:

- **Real Estate Investments:** Real estate investments, such as rental properties or real estate investment trusts (REITs), can generate passive income through rental payments or dividends.

- **Investment Portfolios:** Dividend-paying stocks, bonds, mutual funds, and exchange-traded funds (ETFs) can provide passive income through regular dividends and interest payments.

- **Online Businesses:** Creating and monetizing online content, such as blogs, YouTube channels, e-books, and digital products, can generate passive income through advertising revenue, affiliate marketing, and product sales.

- **Royalties:** Intellectual property, such as books, music, films, and patents, can generate passive income through royalties from sales or licensing agreements.

  - **Peer-to-Peer Lending:** Peer-to-peer lending platforms allow individuals to earn passive income by lending money to borrowers and collecting interest payments.

4. Challenges and Considerations:

  - **Initial Investment:** Some passive income streams may require an initial investment of time, money, or resources to get started.

  - **Risk:** All investments carry some degree of risk, and passive income streams are no exception. It's essential to conduct thorough research and due diligence before investing in any passive income opportunity.

  - **Market Conditions:** Passive income streams may be influenced by economic and market conditions, such as interest rates, inflation, and changes in consumer demand.

- **Maintenance and Management:** While passive income streams require less ongoing effort than active income sources, they still require some level of maintenance and management to ensure they continue to generate income over time.

5. **Diversification and Optimization:**

- Diversifying passive income streams can help mitigate risk and increase overall income stability.

- Continuously optimizing and reinvesting passive income can accelerate wealth growth and maximize returns.

In conclusion, passive income streams offer a powerful way to generate income, build wealth, and achieve financial independence. By diversifying sources of income, creating multiple streams of passive income, and continuously optimizing and reinvesting earnings, individuals can harness the power of passive income to create the lifestyle of their dreams and secure their financial future.

- Investment Strategies for Long-Term Growth

Investment strategies for long-term growth are essential for building wealth, preserving purchasing power, and achieving financial independence over time. These strategies involve allocating capital to assets that have the potential to appreciate and generate returns over an extended period. Here, we comprehensively discuss various investment strategies for long-term growth:

1. **Diversification:** Diversification is a fundamental principle of investing for long-term growth. By spreading investments across different asset classes, industries, and geographical regions, investors can reduce risk and enhance returns. Common asset classes for diversification include stocks, bonds, real estate, commodities, and alternative investments such as private equity and hedge funds.

2. Asset Allocation: Asset allocation involves determining the optimal mix of assets in a portfolio

based on an investor's risk tolerance, investment goals, and time horizon. A well-diversified portfolio typically includes a mix of equities for growth potential, fixed-income securities for income and stability, and alternative investments for diversification and risk management.

3. Stock Market Investing:

- **Long-Term Investing:** Investing in individual stocks or equity mutual funds for the long term can provide exposure to the growth potential of the stock market. Historically, stocks have generated higher returns than other asset classes over the long term, although they also carry higher volatility and risk.

- **Dollar-Cost Averaging:** Dollar-cost averaging involves investing a fixed amount of money at regular intervals, regardless of market conditions. This strategy helps mitigate the impact of market fluctuations and allows investors to accumulate shares over time at various price points.

4. Bond Investing:

- **Government and Corporate Bonds:** Investing in government and corporate bonds can provide fixed-income investors with regular interest payments and principal repayment at maturity. Bonds are typically less volatile than stocks and can provide stability to a diversified portfolio.

- **Bond Funds:** Bond mutual funds or exchange-traded funds (ETFs) offer diversification and professional management for investors seeking exposure to fixed-income securities.

5. Real Estate Investing:

- **Rental Properties:** Investing in rental properties can provide investors with rental income and potential appreciation in property value over time. Real estate investment trusts (REITs) offer an alternative way to invest in real estate without directly owning physical properties.

- **Real Estate Crowdfunding:** Crowdfunding platforms allow investors to pool their capital to invest in real estate projects, offering opportunities for diversification and access to commercial properties and development projects.

6. Retirement Accounts:

- **401(k) and IRA Accounts:** Retirement accounts such as 401(k) plans and individual retirement accounts (IRAs) offer tax advantages and long-term growth potential. Contributing to these accounts regularly and investing in a diversified mix of assets can help investors build wealth for retirement.

7. Tax-Efficient Investing:

- **Tax-Deferred Accounts:** Investing in tax-deferred accounts such as 401(k) plans and IRAs allows investors to defer taxes on investment gains until retirement, potentially maximizing long-term growth.

- **Tax-Efficient Funds:** Investing in tax-efficient mutual funds or ETFs can help minimize tax liabilities and maximize after-tax returns.

8. **Long-Term Perspective:** Successful long-term investors understand the importance of patience, discipline, and a long-term perspective. They resist the temptation to react to short-term market fluctuations and focus on their long-term investment goals.

In conclusion, investment strategies for long-term growth involve diversification, asset allocation, and a disciplined approach to investing. By constructing a well-diversified portfolio, investing regularly, and maintaining a long-term perspective, investors can build wealth, preserve purchasing power, and achieve financial independence over time.

- Entrepreneurship: Building Assets and Creating Value

Entrepreneurship is a dynamic and multifaceted endeavor that involves identifying opportunities, creating value, and building assets to generate wealth and make a positive impact. Entrepreneurs are innovators who leverage their creativity, passion, and resourcefulness to solve problems, meet needs, and capitalize on market opportunities. Here, we comprehensively discuss various aspects of entrepreneurship, including building assets and creating value:

1. **Identifying Opportunities:** Successful entrepreneurs have a keen ability to identify opportunities where others see challenges or problems. This may involve recognizing unmet needs in the market, identifying emerging trends or technologies, or solving existing problems in new and innovative ways. Entrepreneurial opportunities can arise from various sources, including personal experiences, market research, industry trends, and technological advancements.

2. **Creating Value:** At the core of entrepreneurship is the creation of value for customers, stakeholders, and society at large. Value creation involves developing products or services that address

specific needs or pain points, deliver tangible benefits, and provide a unique selling proposition. Successful entrepreneurs focus on understanding their target market, identifying customer preferences and desires, and delivering solutions that exceed expectations.

3. **Building Assets:** Entrepreneurship involves building assets that generate income and create long-term value. These assets may include tangible assets such as physical products, intellectual property such as patents or trademarks, and intangible assets such as brand reputation, customer relationships, and organizational culture. Building assets is essential for creating sustainable businesses and generating wealth over the long term.

4. **Business Models and Revenue Streams:** Entrepreneurs employ various business models and revenue streams to monetize their products or services and generate income. Common business models include selling products or services directly to customers, licensing intellectual property,

franchising, subscription-based models, and advertising-supported models. Diversifying revenue streams can help mitigate risk and maximize profitability.

5. **Innovation and Adaptability:** Entrepreneurship is inherently innovative and adaptive, requiring entrepreneurs to constantly innovate and evolve to stay ahead of the curve. Successful entrepreneurs embrace change, experiment with new ideas, and adapt their strategies based on feedback and market conditions. They are not afraid to take calculated risks and pivot when necessary to seize new opportunities or address emerging challenges.

6. **Risk Management and Resilience:** Entrepreneurship involves inherent risks, including financial risk, market risk, and operational risk. Successful entrepreneurs employ risk management strategies to mitigate these risks and build resilience in their businesses. This may involve conducting thorough market research, developing contingency

plans, diversifying revenue streams, and maintaining strong financial discipline.

7. **Impact and Social Responsibility:** In addition to generating wealth, entrepreneurship offers the opportunity to make a positive impact on society and contribute to the greater good. Socially responsible entrepreneurs prioritize ethical business practices, environmental sustainability, and social impact in their business operations. They aim to create value not only for shareholders but also for employees, customers, and the community at large.

In conclusion, entrepreneurship is a dynamic and transformative force that involves building assets, creating value, and making a positive impact on society. Successful entrepreneurs leverage their creativity, passion, and resourcefulness to identify opportunities, innovate solutions, and build sustainable businesses that generate wealth and create long-term value. By embracing innovation, adaptability, and social responsibility, entrepreneurs can harness the power of entrepreneurship to drive positive change and achieve lasting success.

CHAPTER 3:
FINANCIAL LITERACY AND MANAGEMENT

Financial literacy and management are the cornerstones of personal and financial success. In today's complex and ever-changing economic landscape, the ability to understand and effectively manage one's finances is more critical than ever. Welcome to Chapter 3: Financial Literacy and Management.

In this chapter, we embark on a comprehensive exploration of the fundamental principles of financial literacy and management. From mastering the basics of budgeting and saving to navigating the intricacies of debt management and investment strategies, we delve into the essential knowledge and skills necessary to achieve financial stability and prosperity.

Financial literacy is the foundation upon which sound financial decision-making is built. It involves understanding key financial concepts such as budgeting, saving, investing, borrowing, and protecting against financial risks. By enhancing our financial literacy, we empower ourselves to make informed decisions about money management and wealth building.

Financial management, on the other hand, is the practical application of financial knowledge to manage one's financial affairs effectively. It involves developing strategies and habits to achieve financial goals, prioritize spending, track expenses, and optimize financial resources for maximum efficiency and impact.

Throughout this chapter, we will explore a wide range of topics related to financial literacy and management, including:

1. **Mastering the Basics of Budgeting and Saving:** We discuss the importance of budgeting as a tool

for managing income and expenses, setting financial goals, and controlling spending. We also explore various strategies for saving money, building emergency funds, and planning for future expenses.

2. **Debt Management and Elimination Strategies:** We examine different types of debt, such as credit card debt, student loans, and mortgages, and discuss strategies for managing and reducing debt effectively. We also explore debt consolidation, refinancing, and other techniques for debt elimination.

3. **Maximizing Returns:** Tips for Efficient Money Management: We delve into the principles of efficient money management, including strategies for maximizing returns on investments, minimizing taxes, and optimizing financial resources for long-term growth and prosperity.

4. **Investment Strategies for Long-Term Growth:** We explore various investment strategies for building wealth over time, including asset

allocation, diversification, and risk management. We also discuss different types of investment vehicles, such as stocks, bonds, mutual funds, and real estate.

5. **Financial Planning and Goal Setting:** We emphasize the importance of financial planning and goal setting as essential components of financial management. We discuss how to set SMART (Specific, Measurable, Achievable, Relevant, Time-bound) financial goals and develop actionable plans to achieve them.

By mastering the principles of financial literacy and management outlined in this chapter, you will be equipped with the knowledge and skills necessary to take control of your financial future and achieve your long-term financial goals. Whether you're just starting your financial journey or looking to enhance your existing financial skills, the insights and strategies presented here will provide invaluable guidance on your path to financial stability and prosperity. So, let us embark on this journey together and unlock the keys to financial literacy and management.

- Mastering the Basics of Budgeting and Saving

Mastering the basics of budgeting and saving is foundational to achieving financial stability, building wealth, and reaching long-term financial goals. Budgeting involves creating a plan for how you will allocate your income to cover expenses, save for the future, and achieve your financial objectives. Saving, on the other hand, involves setting aside a portion of your income for future use, emergencies, or specific goals. Here, we comprehensively discuss various aspects of mastering the basics of budgeting and saving:

1. **Understanding Income and Expenses:**

   - **Identify Sources of Income:** Begin by identifying all sources of income, including wages/salary, bonuses, freelance income, investment income, and any other sources of revenue.

- **Track Expenses:** Track all your expenses for a set period (e.g., a month) to understand where your money is going. Categorize expenses into fixed (e.g., rent, mortgage) and variable (e.g., groceries, entertainment) categories.

2. Creating a Budget:

- **Establish Financial Goals:** Define short-term, medium-term, and long-term financial goals, such as paying off debt, saving for a vacation, or building an emergency fund.

- **Allocate Income:** Create a budget that allocates income towards essential expenses (e.g., housing, utilities), discretionary expenses (e.g., dining out, entertainment), savings, and debt repayment.

- **Set Spending Limits:** Set limits on discretionary spending categories to ensure that expenses do not exceed income. Adjust spending as needed to stay within budgetary constraints.

3. Emergency Fund:

- **Importance of Emergency Fund:** Set aside funds in an emergency fund to cover unexpected expenses, such as medical bills, car repairs, or job loss. Aim to build an emergency fund equivalent to three to six months' worth of living expenses.

- **Automate Savings:** Set up automatic transfers from your checking account to your emergency fund to ensure consistent savings.

4. Debt Management:

- **Assess Debt Load:** Evaluate your existing debt obligations, including credit card debt, student loans, and mortgages. Develop a plan to pay off high-interest debt aggressively while maintaining minimum payments on other debts.

- **Debt Snowball or Avalanche:** Consider using the debt snowball method (paying off debts from smallest to largest) or the debt avalanche method (paying off debts from highest to lowest interest rate) to accelerate debt repayment.

5. Savings Goals:

- **Short-Term Goals:** Set short-term savings goals, such as building an emergency fund, saving for a vacation, or making a major purchase.

- **Medium-Term Goals:** Establish medium-term savings goals, such as saving for a down payment on a house, purchasing a car, or funding education expenses.

- **Long-Term Goals:** Define long-term savings goals, such as retirement savings, investing in children's education, or creating a financial legacy.

6. Automate Savings:

- **Pay Yourself First:** Set up automatic transfers from your paycheck to your savings accounts to ensure consistent savings before spending on discretionary expenses.

  - **Use Technology:** Utilize budgeting apps or online banking tools to automate savings, track expenses, and monitor progress towards financial goals.

7. Regular Review and Adjustment:

  - **Review Budget Regularly:** Monitor your budget regularly to track progress towards financial goals and identify areas for improvement.

  - **Adjust as Needed:** Adjust your budget as needed to accommodate changes in income, expenses, or financial priorities.

By mastering the basics of budgeting and saving, you can take control of your finances, reduce financial stress, and work towards achieving your financial aspirations. Whether you're striving to pay off debt, build an emergency fund, save for a major purchase, or invest for the future, effective budgeting and saving habits lay the groundwork for long-term financial success.

- Debt Management and Elimination Strategies

Debt management and elimination strategies are crucial components of achieving financial stability, reducing financial stress, and ultimately building wealth. Effectively managing and eliminating debt involves developing a plan to pay off existing debts efficiently while avoiding accruing additional debt. Here, we comprehensively discuss various aspects of debt management and elimination strategies:

1. **Assessing Debt Load:**

   - **Take Inventory:** Begin by compiling a comprehensive list of all outstanding debts, including credit card balances, student loans, car loans, personal loans, and mortgages.

   - **Understand Terms:** Review the terms of each debt, including interest rates, minimum monthly payments, and repayment schedules.

2. **Creating a Debt Repayment Plan:**

- **Debt Snowball Method:** The debt snowball method involves paying off debts in order from smallest to largest balance while making minimum payments on all other debts. As each debt is paid off, the freed-up funds are applied to the next debt on the list.

- **Debt Avalanche Method:** The debt avalanche method involves paying off debts in order from highest to lowest interest rate while making minimum payments on all other debts. This approach minimizes the total interest paid over time.

- **Hybrid Approach:** Some individuals may prefer a hybrid approach that combines elements of both the debt snowball and debt avalanche methods, prioritizing debts based on a combination of balance and interest rate.

3. Increasing Debt Repayment Efforts:

- **Allocate Additional Funds:** Look for ways to free up additional funds to accelerate debt repayment, such as cutting discretionary expenses, increasing income through side hustles or part-time work, or reallocating windfalls such as tax refunds or bonuses.

- **Make Extra Payments:** Apply any extra funds towards debt repayment, such as making biweekly payments instead of monthly payments or using unexpected windfalls to make lump-sum payments towards principal.

4. Negotiating with Creditors:

- **Interest Rate Reduction:** Contact creditors to inquire about lowering interest rates on existing debts, especially credit card balances. A lower interest rate can reduce the total cost of borrowing and accelerate debt repayment.

- **Debt Settlement:** Consider negotiating with creditors to settle debts for less than the full amount owed, particularly for unsecured debts such as credit card debt. Debt settlement may result in a lower total payoff amount but can have negative consequences for credit scores.

5. Consolidating Debt:

- **Balance Transfer:** Consider transferring high-interest credit card balances to a new credit card with a lower promotional interest rate or a balance transfer offer. Be mindful of balance transfer fees and the duration of the promotional period.

- **Debt Consolidation Loan:** Explore the option of consolidating multiple debts into a single loan with a lower interest rate and a fixed repayment term. Debt consolidation can simplify debt repayment and potentially reduce overall interest costs.

6. Avoiding Future Debt:

- **Budgeting and Planning:** Develop a budget and spending plan to live within your means and avoid overspending. Allocate funds towards savings goals and discretionary expenses while prioritizing debt repayment.

- **Emergency Fund:** Build an emergency fund to cover unexpected expenses and financial emergencies, reducing the need to rely on credit cards or loans in times of need.

7. Seeking Professional Help:

- **Credit Counseling:** Consider working with a nonprofit credit counseling agency to develop a personalized debt repayment plan and receive guidance on managing finances responsibly.

- **Debt Management Plan:** Explore the option of enrolling in a debt management plan (DMP) through a credit counseling agency, which may negotiate with creditors on your behalf to lower interest rates and consolidate debts into a single monthly payment.

In conclusion, effective debt management and elimination strategies involve developing a comprehensive plan to pay off existing debts efficiently while avoiding accruing additional debt. By assessing debt load, creating a debt repayment plan, increasing debt repayment efforts, negotiating with creditors, consolidating debt, avoiding future debt, and seeking professional help when needed, individuals can take control of their finances, reduce financial stress, and work towards achieving long-term financial stability and freedom.

- Maximizing Returns: Tips for Efficient Money Management

Maximizing returns through efficient money management involves optimizing the use of financial resources to achieve the highest possible return on investment while minimizing risks and expenses. Effective money management strategies allow individuals to grow wealth, achieve financial goals, and secure their financial future. Here, we comprehensively discuss various tips for maximizing returns through efficient money management:

1. **Set Clear Financial Goals:**

- **Define Objectives:** Start by setting clear and specific financial goals, such as saving for retirement, buying a home, funding education, or building an emergency fund.

- **Prioritize Goals:** Prioritize goals based on importance, urgency, and feasibility, and allocate financial resources accordingly.

2. **Develop a Comprehensive Financial Plan:**

- **Budgeting:** Create a detailed budget that outlines income, expenses, and savings goals. Track spending, identify areas for improvement, and adjust the budget as needed.

- **Emergency Fund:** Build an emergency fund to cover unexpected expenses and financial emergencies, aiming for three to six months' worth of living expenses.

- **Debt Management:** Develop a plan to pay off existing debts efficiently while avoiding accruing additional debt. Consider using strategies such as the debt snowball or debt avalanche method to accelerate debt repayment.

3. Invest Wisely:

- **Asset Allocation:** Diversify investments across different asset classes, such as stocks, bonds, real estate, and cash equivalents, to reduce risk and maximize returns. Consider factors such as risk tolerance, investment horizon, and financial goals when determining asset allocation.

- **Risk Management:** Assess risk tolerance and invest by risk tolerance levels. Consider factors such as investment objectives, time horizon, and financial situation when evaluating risk.

- **Regular Review:** Monitor investment portfolios regularly and rebalance as needed to maintain desired asset allocation and risk levels. Consider adjusting investments based on changes in market conditions, economic outlook, and personal circumstances.

4. Minimize Expenses and Fees:

- **Cost Awareness:** Be mindful of investment expenses, such as management fees, transaction costs, and fund expenses. Choose low-cost investment options, such as index funds or exchange-traded funds (ETFs), to minimize fees and expenses.

- **Fee Comparison:** Compare fees and expenses across investment options to identify cost-effective solutions. Consider factors such as expense ratios, trading costs, and tax implications when evaluating investment options.

- **Tax Efficiency:** Optimize tax efficiency by investing in tax-advantaged accounts, such as employer-sponsored retirement plans (e.g., 401(k) or 403(b) plans), individual retirement accounts (IRAs), or health savings accounts (HSAs). Consider tax implications when making investment decisions and explore tax-saving strategies, such as tax-loss harvesting or retirement account contributions.

5. Maximize Income:

- **Additional Income Streams:** Explore opportunities to increase income through side hustles, freelance work, rental income, or passive income streams. Identify skills, talents, or assets that can be monetized to generate additional revenue.

 - **Career Development**: Invest in education, training, or professional development to enhance skills, qualifications, and earning potential. Pursue opportunities for career advancement, promotions, or higher-paying job opportunities.

6. **Continuous Learning and Improvement:**

 - **Stay Informed:** Stay informed about financial markets, investment trends, and economic developments through reputable sources such as financial news websites, books, podcasts, or professional advisors.

 - **Financial Education:** Invest in financial education and literacy to improve knowledge, skills, and confidence in managing finances effectively.

Attend workshops, seminars, or courses on personal finance, investing, and money management.

7. Seek Professional Advice When Needed:

- **Financial Advisor**: Consider seeking advice from a qualified financial advisor or planner to develop a personalized financial plan tailored to individual goals, risk tolerance, and financial situation. Evaluate credentials, experience, and expertise when selecting a financial advisor.

- **Legal and Tax Advice:** Consult legal and tax professionals for guidance on estate planning, tax strategies, asset protection, or other complex financial matters. Ensure compliance with applicable laws, regulations, and tax requirements.

By implementing these tips for efficient money management, individuals can maximize returns, minimize risks, and achieve their financial goals effectively. Whether building wealth, saving for retirement, or planning for major life events, efficient money management strategies lay the foundation for financial success and security.

CHAPTER 4: LIFESTYLE DESIGN AND ABUNDANCE

In the pursuit of holistic well-being and fulfillment, lifestyle design and abundance play integral roles. Beyond mere financial success, true abundance encompasses richness in all aspects of life – from health and relationships to personal growth and fulfillment. Welcome to Chapter 4: Lifestyle Design and Abundance.

In this chapter, we embark on a transformative exploration of how intentional lifestyle design can lead to a life of abundance, joy, and purpose. We delve into the principles of conscious living, intentional decision-making, and aligning actions with values to create a life that reflects our deepest desires and aspirations.

Lifestyle design is not just about the accumulation of material wealth or possessions; it's about crafting a life that resonates with our unique vision of abundance and fulfillment. It involves consciously designing our daily routines, habits, and environments to support our goals, values, and well-being.

Abundance, in this context, goes beyond financial prosperity to encompass a mindset of gratitude, generosity, and abundance in all areas of life. It's about cultivating a sense of abundance in relationships, health, creativity, and personal growth – recognizing the infinite possibilities available to us when we align with the flow of life.

Throughout this chapter, we will explore a wide range of topics related to lifestyle design and abundance, including:

1. **Clarifying Values and Priorities:** We discuss the importance of clarifying our values and priorities to guide decision-making and ensure that

our actions align with our deepest desires and aspirations.

2. **Creating a Vision for Abundance:** We explore techniques for creating a compelling vision for abundance in all areas of life – from health and relationships to career and personal growth.

3. **Mindset Mastery:** We delve into the power of mindset in shaping our experiences and perceptions of abundance. We discuss strategies for cultivating a mindset of abundance, gratitude, and positivity, even in the face of challenges or setbacks.

4. **Intentional Living:** We examine the principles of intentional living and deliberate decision-making. We explore techniques for simplifying our lives, minimizing distractions, and focusing on what truly matters to us.

5. **Practices for Cultivating Abundance:** We discuss practical tools and practices for cultivating abundance in daily life, such as mindfulness, meditation, visualization, and gratitude journaling.

6. **Creating Abundance in Relationships:** We explore the role of relationships in fostering abundance and well-being. We discuss strategies for nurturing meaningful connections, setting boundaries, and cultivating supportive networks.

7. **Living in Alignment with Purpose:** We discuss the importance of living in alignment with our purpose and passions. We explore ways to identify our unique gifts and talents and leverage them to create a life of meaning, purpose, and fulfillment.

By embracing the principles of lifestyle design and abundance outlined in this chapter, you will be empowered to create a life that reflects your deepest values, desires, and aspirations. Whether you're seeking greater fulfillment, joy, or purpose, the insights and strategies presented here will provide invaluable guidance on your journey to a life of abundance and well-being. So, let us embark on this transformative journey together and unlock the keys to lifestyle design and abundance.

- Defining Your Personal Vision of Prosperity

Defining your vision of prosperity is a transformative process that involves clarifying your values, identifying your aspirations, and envisioning the life you want to create for yourself. True prosperity extends beyond material wealth to encompass fulfillment, joy, purpose, and well-being in all aspects of life. Here, we comprehensively discuss the steps and considerations involved in defining your vision of prosperity:

1. **Reflect on Your Values and Priorities:**

   - Begin by reflecting on your core values and priorities. What truly matters to you in life? Consider aspects such as relationships, health, personal growth, career, spirituality, and community involvement.

- Identify the values that resonate most deeply
with you and prioritize them based on their
significance in shaping your life and decisions.

2. Envision Your Ideal Life:

- Imagine your ideal life in vivid detail. What
does prosperity look like to you? Visualize various
aspects of your life, including your career,
relationships, health, finances, lifestyle, and
personal development.

- Consider how you would spend your time,
where you would live, who you would surround
yourself with, and what activities would bring you
joy and fulfillment.

3. Set Specific Goals and Milestones:

- Break down your vision of prosperity into
specific, actionable goals and milestones. What
steps can you take to move closer to your ideal life?
Set SMART (Specific, Measurable, Achievable,
Relevant, Time-bound) goals that align with your
vision and values.

- Prioritize your goals based on their importance and feasibility, and create a plan to achieve them over time.

4. Consider Different Dimensions of Prosperity:

- **Financial Prosperity:** Consider your financial goals and aspirations, such as achieving financial independence, building wealth, or pursuing a career that aligns with your passions and values.

- **Emotional Well-being:** Reflect on your emotional health and well-being. What practices and habits contribute to your overall happiness and fulfillment? Consider aspects such as self-care, stress management, and cultivating positive relationships.

- **Physical Health:** Prioritize your physical health and well-being by setting goals related to nutrition, exercise, sleep, and overall lifestyle habits.

- **Personal Growth:** Embrace opportunities for personal growth and development. Set goals to expand your knowledge, skills, and experiences, and pursue activities that challenge and inspire you.

- **Relationships:** Cultivate meaningful connections and relationships with family, friends, colleagues, and community members. Set goals to nurture these relationships and create a supportive network of individuals who uplift and empower you.

- **Contribution and Impact:** Consider how you can make a positive impact in the world and contribute to causes that are meaningful to you. Set goals to give back to your community, volunteer, or advocate for social and environmental causes.

5. **Review and Revise Regularly:**

- Regularly review and revise your vision of prosperity to ensure that it remains aligned with your evolving values, aspirations, and life circumstances.

- Celebrate your progress and accomplishments along the way, and be open to adjusting your goals and priorities as needed.

6. Seek Alignment and Integration:

- Strive for alignment and integration across different areas of your life. Ensure that your goals and actions are congruent with your values and contribute to your overall sense of prosperity and well-being.

- Identify areas where there may be conflicts or discrepancies between your values and actions, and make adjustments to bring them into harmony.

By defining your vision of prosperity and aligning your goals and actions with your values and aspirations, you can create a life that is truly fulfilling, meaningful, and abundant in all dimensions. Embrace the journey of self-discovery and empowerment as you work towards manifesting your vision of prosperity in the world.

- Cultivating a Lifestyle Aligned with Your Values

Cultivating a lifestyle aligned with your values is essential for achieving a sense of fulfillment, purpose, and well-being. When your actions, choices, and priorities reflect your core values, you experience greater authenticity, satisfaction, and harmony in all aspects of life. Here, we comprehensively discuss the process and principles of cultivating a lifestyle aligned with your values:

1. **Identify Your Core Values:**

   - Begin by identifying your core values – the principles and beliefs that are most important to you. Reflect on what matters most in your life, what motivates you, and what gives you a sense of meaning and purpose.

   - Common values may include integrity, honesty, compassion, resilience, creativity, freedom, justice, spirituality, and connection with others.

2. Clarify Your Priorities:

- Once you've identified your core values, clarify your priorities based on their significance in shaping your life and decisions. Consider which values are non-negotiable and which may require more attention or development.

- Prioritize your values based on their alignment with your long-term goals, aspirations, and vision for your life.

3. Align Your Actions with Your Values:

- Evaluate your current lifestyle and behaviors to assess how well they align with your values. Identify areas where there may be discrepancies or conflicts between your values and actions.

- Make conscious choices and decisions that honor your values in all areas of your life, including relationships, career, health, finances, leisure activities, and personal development.

4. Set Goals and Intentions:

- Set goals and intentions that reflect your values and priorities. Define specific, actionable steps you can take to cultivate a lifestyle that aligns with your values and moves you closer to your desired outcomes.

- Use your values as a guiding framework for setting goals, making decisions, and navigating life's challenges and opportunities.

5. Create Daily Rituals and Habits:

- Cultivate daily rituals and habits that reinforce your values and support your well-being. Incorporate activities and practices that resonate with your values, such as mindfulness meditation, journaling, exercise, creativity, or acts of kindness.

- Establish routines that promote balance, self-care, and personal growth, and eliminate habits that are incongruent with your values or detract from your overall well-being.

6. Surround Yourself with Like-Minded Individuals:

- Surround yourself with people who share similar values and beliefs. Cultivate relationships with individuals who inspire, support, and encourage you to live authentically and in alignment with your values.

- Seek out communities, groups, or organizations that resonate with your values and provide opportunities for connection, collaboration, and shared growth.

7. Practice Mindful Decision-Making:

- Practice mindful decision-making by considering how each choice aligns with your values and contributes to your overall well-being and fulfillment. Pause and reflect before making decisions, and choose actions that honor your values and serve your highest good.

- Be willing to make difficult decisions or sacrifices to maintain alignment with your values,

even if it means stepping outside your comfort zone
or challenging societal norms.

8. **Regularly Review and Adjust:**

- Regularly review your lifestyle, goals, and
priorities to ensure they remain aligned with your
values and aspirations. Reflect on your progress,
celebrate successes, and identify areas for growth or
refinement.

- Be open to adjusting your goals, habits, and
routines as needed to stay true to your values and
continue evolving on your journey of personal
growth and self-discovery.

By cultivating a lifestyle aligned with your values,
you create a sense of authenticity, purpose, and
fulfillment that enriches every aspect of your life.
Embrace the journey of self-awareness and
intentional living as you strive to create a life that
reflects your deepest values and aspirations.

- The Art of Manifestation: Turning Dreams into Reality

The art of manifestation is a transformative practice that involves harnessing the power of intention, belief, and alignment to turn dreams into reality. Manifestation is based on the principle that our thoughts, beliefs, and emotions can shape our external reality and create the outcomes we desire. By consciously directing our energy and focus towards our goals, we can attract opportunities, resources, and experiences that align with our deepest desires. Here, we comprehensively discuss the principles and techniques of the art of manifestation:

1. **Clarify Your Vision:**

- Begin by clarifying your vision and defining what you want to manifest in your life. Be specific and detailed about your goals, aspirations, and desires. Visualize yourself already experiencing your desired outcomes with vivid detail and emotional intensity.

- Use visualization techniques to create mental images of your desired reality, imagining yourself achieving your goals and living the life you desire.

2. Set Clear Intentions:

- Set clear and specific intentions for what you want to manifest. Write down your intentions in the present tense as if they have already been achieved. Affirm your intentions regularly through positive affirmations, visualizations, or written statements.

- Focus on the feelings and emotions associated with your desired outcomes, infusing your intentions with a sense of gratitude, joy, and abundance.

3. Believe in Yourself and Your Dreams:

- Cultivate unwavering belief in yourself and your ability to manifest your desires. Trust in the inherent power of your thoughts and emotions to shape your reality. Release doubts, fears, and limiting beliefs that may be holding you back from achieving your goals.

- Affirm your worthiness and deservingness of your desires, recognizing that you are capable of creating the life you desire.

4. Practice Positive Thinking and Affirmations:

- Cultivate a positive mindset by focusing on thoughts and beliefs that support your goals and aspirations. Replace negative self-talk and self-doubt with positive affirmations and empowering beliefs.

- Affirmations are positive statements that affirm your desired outcomes and reinforce your belief in their attainment. Repeat affirmations regularly with conviction and emotion to reinforce their impact on your subconscious mind.

5. Align Your Actions with Your Intentions:

- Take inspired action towards your goals and intentions. Act as if your desires are already manifesting in your life and make choices that align with your vision.

- Trust your intuition and follow inner guidance as you take steps towards your goals. Be open to opportunities, synchronicities, and signs that may guide you on your path.

6. Practice Gratitude and Appreciation:

- Cultivate an attitude of gratitude and appreciation for the blessings and abundance in your life. Focus on what you already have and express gratitude for the progress you've made towards your goals.

- Gratitude is a powerful force that amplifies the energy of manifestation and attracts more blessings and abundance into your life. Regularly express gratitude through journaling, meditation, or verbal affirmations.

7. Release Attachment to Outcomes:

- Release attachment to specific outcomes and trust in the divine timing and unfolding of events.

Detach from the how and when of manifestation, and surrender to the greater intelligence of the universe.

- Trust that the universe is working in your favor and that everything is unfolding according to a higher plan. Let go of resistance and surrender to the flow of life.

8. Stay Consistent and Persistent:

- Stay consistent and persistent in your practice of manifestation. Maintain a daily routine of visualization, affirmation, and inspired action towards your goals.

- Be patient and trust in the process of manifestation, knowing that your desires are on their way to you. Stay focused on the result and keep moving forward with faith and determination.

9. Celebrate Successes and Acknowledge Progress:

- Celebrate successes and milestones along the way, no matter how small. Acknowledge the progress you've made towards your goals and celebrate each step forward.

- Cultivate a sense of joy and appreciation for the manifestations that have already occurred in your life, and use them as evidence of your ability to create the life you desire.

10. **Stay Open to Receive:**

- Stay open and receptive to the abundance of the universe. Be open to receiving blessings, opportunities, and manifestations in unexpected ways and from unexpected sources.

- Trust that the universe is conspiring to support you in manifesting your desires, and remain open to miracles and blessings that may come your way.

By practicing the art of manifestation, you can harness the power of your thoughts, beliefs, and intentions to create the life of your dreams. Through clarity, intention, belief, alignment, and inspired action, you can turn your dreams into reality and manifest the abundance, joy, and fulfillment you deserve. Embrace the journey of manifestation with faith, trust, and gratitude, knowing that you have the power to create the life you desire.

CHAPTER 5: LEGACY, IMPACT, AND CONTRIBUTION

Welcome to Chapter 5: Legacy, Impact, and Contribution. In this chapter, we embark on a journey of exploration into the profound concepts of legacy, impact, and contribution. While prosperity often begins with personal fulfillment and financial success, it extends far beyond individual achievements to encompass the lasting imprint we leave on the world and the lives of others.

Legacy, impact, and contribution are timeless themes that resonate deeply with the human experience. They prompt us to reflect on the mark we wish to leave on the world, the difference we aspire to make in the lives of others, and the values we hope to instill in future generations. Whether through acts of kindness, creative expression, philanthropy, or social change, each of us has the power to shape our legacy and leave a lasting impact on the world.

In this chapter, we will delve into the multifaceted dimensions of legacy, impact, and contribution, exploring topics such as:

1. **Defining Your Legacy:** We will discuss the concept of legacy and its significance in shaping our sense of identity, purpose, and fulfillment. We will explore techniques for clarifying and articulating the legacy we wish to leave behind, considering both personal and professional aspirations.

2. **Making a Difference:** We will examine the power of impact and contribution in creating positive change in the world. We will explore ways to identify opportunities for making a difference, whether through volunteer work, philanthropy, activism, or social entrepreneurship.

3. **Creating Meaningful Connections:** We will discuss the importance of fostering meaningful connections and relationships as a cornerstone of legacy and impact. We will explore strategies for

building authentic connections with others, fostering empathy and compassion, and nurturing supportive communities.

4. **Leaving a Lasting Legacy:** We will explore strategies for leaving a lasting legacy that extends beyond individual achievements to create a ripple effect of positive change. We will examine the role of values, ethics, and integrity in shaping our legacy, and discuss ways to inspire and empower others to carry forward our vision and values.

5. **Measuring Impact:** We will discuss techniques for measuring and evaluating the impact of our actions and contributions. We will explore both quantitative and qualitative methods for assessing the effectiveness of our efforts and identifying opportunities for improvement and innovation.

6. **Sustainability and Stewardship:** We will explore the importance of sustainability and stewardship in shaping our legacy and impact. We will discuss ways to promote environmental sustainability, social responsibility, and ethical

leadership in our personal and professional endeavors.

7. **Celebrating and Honoring Legacies:** We will discuss the importance of celebrating and honoring the legacies of others, recognizing the contributions of past generations, and preserving cultural heritage and traditions for future generations.

By exploring the themes of legacy, impact, and contribution in this chapter, we will gain a deeper understanding of our role in shaping the world and the importance of leaving a positive mark on the lives of others. Whether through acts of kindness, creativity, leadership, or service, each of us has the power to make a meaningful difference and leave a lasting legacy that inspires and uplifts future generations. So, let us embark on this journey of exploration and discovery, as we explore the profound themes of legacy, impact, and contribution.

- Beyond Personal Wealth: Leveraging Prosperity for Good

Beyond personal wealth lies a profound opportunity to leverage prosperity for the greater good, to create positive change in the world and to uplift communities. While personal wealth can bring comfort and security, true fulfillment often comes from using our resources, influence, and privilege to make a meaningful impact on the lives of others and contribute to the betterment of society. In this comprehensive discussion, we will explore the various ways in which individuals can leverage their prosperity for good:

1. **Philanthropy and Charitable Giving:**

   - Philanthropy involves donating money, time, or resources to charitable causes and organizations that address pressing social, environmental, or humanitarian issues.

- Individuals can leverage their financial resources to support causes they are passionate about, whether it's education, healthcare, poverty alleviation, environmental conservation, or social justice.

- Philanthropic efforts can range from one-time donations to establishing charitable foundations or endowments that provide sustained support to worthy causes over time.

2. Social Entrepreneurship and Impact Investing:

- Social entrepreneurship involves using entrepreneurial principles and business strategies to address social or environmental challenges while generating financial returns.

- Impact investing refers to investing in companies, organizations, or funds to generate positive social or environmental impact alongside financial returns.

- Individuals can leverage their entrepreneurial skills, expertise, and financial resources to launch or support social enterprises and impact-driven businesses that create sustainable solutions to pressing global issues.

3. **Advocacy and Activism:**

   - Advocacy involves using one's voice, influence, and platform to raise awareness, promote social change, and advocate for policies that address systemic injustices or inequities.

   - Individuals can leverage their influence as thought leaders, influencers, or public figures to advocate for causes they believe in, whether it's climate action, human rights, gender equality, or racial justice.

   - Engaging in grassroots activism, community organizing, or political advocacy can also be a powerful way to leverage prosperity for good by mobilizing collective action and driving social change.

4. **Corporate Social Responsibility (CSR):**

- Corporate social responsibility (CSR) involves integrating social and environmental considerations into business operations and decision-making processes.

- Companies and organizations can leverage their financial resources, expertise, and influence to support community development initiatives, environmental conservation efforts, and social impact projects.

- Individuals in leadership positions within companies can advocate for CSR initiatives and champion ethical business practices that prioritize social and environmental impact alongside profitability.

5. Volunteerism and Community Engagement:

- Volunteering involves donating time, skills, and expertise to support local communities, nonprofits, and grassroots organizations.

- Individuals can leverage their time and talents to volunteer for causes they care about, whether it's mentoring youth, serving meals at homeless shelters, or organizing community clean-up events.

- Engaging in community service and volunteerism not only benefits others but also fosters a sense of connection, empathy, and purpose.

6. Education and Capacity Building:

- Education and capacity-building initiatives empower individuals and communities with the knowledge, skills, and resources they need to thrive.

- Individuals can leverage their expertise, networks, and resources to support education initiatives, vocational training programs, and capacity-building projects that empower marginalized communities and promote economic opportunity.

- Mentoring, coaching, and skills-based volunteering are effective ways to share knowledge and empower others to reach their full potential.

7. **Environmental Stewardship and Sustainable Practices:**

- Environmental stewardship involves taking responsibility for the care and preservation of the natural environment and adopting sustainable practices that minimize ecological impact.

- Individuals can leverage their influence as consumers, investors, and citizens to support sustainable businesses, advocate for environmental policies, and adopt eco-friendly habits in their daily lives.

- Investing in renewable energy, reducing carbon emissions, conserving natural resources, and supporting conservation efforts are all ways to leverage prosperity for the greater good of the planet and future generations.

8. **Global Solidarity and Humanitarian Aid:**

- Global solidarity involves standing in solidarity with communities around the world facing adversity, crisis, or injustice, and providing humanitarian aid and support.

- Individuals can leverage their resources to support international development organizations, humanitarian relief efforts, and disaster response initiatives that provide lifesaving assistance to those in need.

- Supporting refugees, displaced persons, and vulnerable populations affected by conflict, poverty, or natural disasters is an essential way to leverage prosperity for good and promote global solidarity.

9. Cultural Preservation and Arts Patronage:

- Cultural preservation involves safeguarding and promoting the rich cultural heritage, traditions, and artistic expressions of diverse communities.

- Individuals can leverage their resources to support cultural institutions, museums, libraries, and arts organizations that preserve and celebrate cultural diversity and artistic excellence.

- Patronizing artists, artisans, and cultural practitioners, and supporting cultural exchange programs and heritage conservation projects are meaningful ways to leverage prosperity for the preservation and promotion of cultural heritage.

In conclusion, leveraging prosperity for good goes beyond personal enrichment to create positive change in the world and uplift communities. Whether through philanthropy, social entrepreneurship, advocacy, volunteerism, education, environmental stewardship, global solidarity, cultural preservation, or other forms of contribution, individuals have the power to make a meaningful impact and leave a lasting legacy of compassion, generosity, and service. By aligning personal values with actions that benefit others and the planet, individuals can leverage their prosperity for the greater good and contribute to building a more just, equitable, and sustainable world for present and future generations.

- Creating a Lasting Legacy Through Generosity and Philanthropy

Creating a lasting legacy through generosity and philanthropy is a transformative act that extends beyond personal wealth to positively impact individuals, communities, and society as a whole. By leveraging financial resources, influence, and passion for social good, individuals can leave a lasting imprint on the world and inspire others to follow in their footsteps. In this comprehensive discussion, we will explore the principles, benefits, and strategies for creating a lasting legacy through generosity and philanthropy:

1. **Principles of Generosity and Philanthropy:**

   - Generosity and philanthropy are rooted in the principles of compassion, empathy, and altruism, driven by a desire to make a positive difference in the lives of others.

- At its core, philanthropy involves the voluntary giving of resources, whether financial, time, skills, or expertise, to support charitable causes and address pressing social, environmental, or humanitarian issues.

- Philanthropy is guided by values such as integrity, transparency, accountability, and impact, with a focus on creating sustainable solutions and empowering individuals and communities to thrive.

2. Benefits of Creating a Lasting Legacy Through Generosity and Philanthropy:

- **Personal Fulfillment:** Engaging in acts of generosity and philanthropy brings a sense of fulfillment, purpose, and meaning to one's life, as individuals witness the positive impact of their contributions on others.

- **Positive Impact:** Philanthropy has the power to create lasting change by addressing systemic injustices, promoting social equality, and improving the quality of life for vulnerable populations.

- **Social Connection:** Generosity and philanthropy foster a sense of connection and community by bringing people together around shared values and common goals, inspiring collaboration and collective action.

- **Legacy and Immortality:** By creating a lasting legacy through generosity and philanthropy, individuals ensure that their values, beliefs, and contributions continue to make a difference long after they are gone, leaving a positive imprint on future generations.

3. Strategies for Creating a Lasting Legacy Through Generosity and Philanthropy:

- **Identify Your Passion and Purpose:** Start by identifying causes and issues that resonate deeply with your values, interests, and life experiences. Consider how you can leverage your resources and expertise to make a meaningful impact in these areas.

- Set Clear Goals and Objectives: Define specific goals and objectives for your philanthropic endeavors, outlining what you hope to achieve and how you plan to measure success. Consider both short-term and long-term outcomes, and prioritize initiatives that align with your overarching vision for creating a lasting legacy.

- Develop a Strategic Giving Plan: Develop a strategic giving plan that outlines your philanthropic priorities, target beneficiaries, funding strategies, and allocation of resources. Consider factors such as budget, timing, geography, and impact measurement when designing your giving strategy.

- Collaborate and Partner with Others: Explore opportunities for collaboration and partnership with like-minded individuals, organizations, corporations, and government agencies. By pooling resources and expertise, you can amplify the impact of your philanthropic efforts and achieve greater results.

- **Embrace Innovation and Creativity:** Be open to innovative approaches and creative solutions to complex social challenges. Explore new technologies, models, and strategies that have the potential to drive systemic change and create lasting impact in your chosen areas of focus.

- **Engage in Hands-On Involvement:** In addition to financial contributions, consider ways to actively engage in hands-on involvement and direct service with the causes and organizations you support. Volunteer your time, skills, and expertise to make a tangible difference in the lives of others and deepen your understanding of the issues at hand.

- **Foster Transparency and Accountability:** Foster transparency and accountability in your philanthropic endeavors by communicating openly with stakeholders, sharing information about your activities and impact, and upholding high ethical standards in all aspects of your work.

- **Evaluate and Adapt Over Time:** Continuously evaluate the effectiveness of your philanthropic efforts and be willing to adapt and refine your approach based on lessons learned and changing circumstances. Regularly review your goals, assess your progress, and make adjustments as needed to maximize your impact and create a lasting legacy of generosity and philanthropy.

In conclusion, creating a lasting legacy through generosity and philanthropy is a noble and transformative endeavor that has the power to change lives, communities, and society for the better. By embracing the principles of generosity, compassion, and social responsibility, individuals can leave a positive imprint on the world and inspire others to join them in the pursuit of a more just, equitable, and compassionate world for all. Whether through financial contributions, volunteerism, advocacy, or hands-on involvement, each act of generosity and philanthropy has the potential to create a ripple effect of positive change that reverberates far into the future, leaving a legacy of hope, opportunity, and dignity for generations to come.

- Making a Meaningful Impact: Finding Purpose Beyond Profit

Making a meaningful impact involves finding purpose beyond profit and leveraging one's skills, resources, and influence to create positive change in the world. It entails aligning personal values with actions that contribute to the greater good, whether through philanthropy, social entrepreneurship, advocacy, volunteerism, or other forms of social impact. In this comprehensive discussion, we will explore the principles, benefits, and strategies for making a meaningful impact and finding purpose beyond profit:

1. Understanding the Importance of Purpose and Meaning:

- Purpose and meaning are fundamental human needs that transcend material wealth and external success. They involve a sense of fulfillment,

contribution, and connection to something larger
than oneself.

- Research has shown that individuals who derive
a sense of purpose from their work and lives are
happier, healthier, and more resilient in the face of
challenges. They experience greater levels of
satisfaction, engagement, and well-being.

2. **Recognizing the Power of Impact and
Contribution:**

- Impact and contribution involve using one's
skills, resources, and influence to make a positive
difference in the lives of others and the world at
large.

- Making a meaningful impact goes beyond
personal gain or recognition; it involves creating
lasting change that benefits individuals,
communities, and society as a whole.

3. **Embracing Values-Driven Decision-Making:**

- Values-driven decision-making involves aligning actions and choices with personal values, beliefs, and principles.

- By prioritizing values such as compassion, empathy, integrity, and social responsibility, individuals can ensure that their actions contribute to the greater good and reflect their commitment to making a meaningful impact.

4. **Exploring Pathways to Social Impact:**

- There are numerous pathways to social impact, including philanthropy, social entrepreneurship, advocacy, volunteerism, and corporate social responsibility.

- Philanthropy involves donating money, time, or resources to support charitable causes and address pressing social, environmental, or humanitarian issues.

- Social entrepreneurship combines business principles with a social mission to create innovative solutions to social and environmental challenges while generating financial returns.

- Advocacy involves using one's voice, influence, and platform to raise awareness, promote social change, and advocate for policies that address systemic injustices or inequities.

- Volunteerism entails donating time, skills, and expertise to support local communities, nonprofits, and grassroots organizations.

- Corporate social responsibility (CSR) involves integrating social and environmental considerations into business operations and decision-making processes.

5. Setting Goals and Measuring Impact:

- Setting clear goals and objectives is essential for making a meaningful impact. Define specific outcomes you hope to achieve and develop strategies for measuring progress and evaluating success.

   - Consider both short-term and long-term impact metrics, such as the number of lives impacted, improvements in quality of life, or systemic changes in policy or practice.

6. Building Collaborative Partnerships:

   - Collaboration and partnership are essential for maximizing social impact. By working together with like-minded individuals, organizations, corporations, and government agencies, individuals can leverage collective expertise, resources, and networks to achieve common goals.

   - Foster collaboration through strategic alliances, joint initiatives, and shared learning opportunities that amplify the reach and effectiveness of social impact efforts.

7. Fostering Innovation and Creativity:

   - Innovation and creativity are key drivers of social impact. Encourage innovative thinking and experimentation to develop new solutions to complex social and environmental challenges.

- Embrace a culture of learning, adaptation, and continuous improvement to stay agile and responsive to evolving needs and opportunities.

8. Practicing Self-Care and Well-Being:

- Making a meaningful impact can be emotionally and physically demanding. It's essential to prioritize self-care and well-being to maintain resilience, balance, and effectiveness.

- Incorporate practices such as mindfulness, meditation, exercise, and time spent in nature to recharge and replenish your energy.

9. Celebrating Successes and Acknowledging Challenges:

- Celebrate successes and milestones along the way, no matter how small. Acknowledge the progress you've made and the positive impact you've had on individuals and communities.

- Recognize that making a meaningful impact is a journey filled with ups and downs, setbacks, and challenges. Embrace failures as learning opportunities and remain resilient in the face of adversity.

10. Inspiring and Empowering Others:

- Use your platform and influence to inspire and empower others to join you in making a meaningful impact. Share your experiences, insights, and lessons learned to encourage others to find their paths to social impact.

- Mentorship, coaching, and leadership development are powerful tools for nurturing the next generation of change-makers and equipping them with the skills and resources they need to create positive change in their communities and beyond.

In conclusion, making a meaningful impact involves finding purpose beyond profit and leveraging one's skills, resources, and influence to create positive change in the world. By aligning personal values with actions that contribute to the greater good, individuals can experience a sense of fulfillment, connection, and purpose that transcends material wealth and external success. Whether through philanthropy, social entrepreneurship, advocacy, volunteerism, or other forms of social impact, each individual has the power to make a difference and leave a lasting legacy of compassion, generosity, and social responsibility. Let us embrace the journey of making a meaningful impact and inspire others to join us in creating a better world for all.

CONCLUSION

In conclusion, "The Prosperity Paradigm: Unlocking Wealth and Securing Financial Freedom" has been a journey of exploration and empowerment, guiding readers towards a holistic understanding of prosperity and its multifaceted dimensions. Throughout these pages, we've delved into the psychology of wealth, the mindset of prosperity, and the practical strategies for achieving financial freedom. We've explored the power of passive income streams, investment strategies for long-term growth, and the principles of entrepreneurship. We've delved into the essentials of financial literacy, mastering budgeting, saving, debt management, and efficient money management. We've also examined the profound themes of legacy, impact, and contribution, urging readers to leverage their prosperity for the greater good and leave a lasting legacy of compassion, generosity, and social responsibility.

As we conclude this journey, I invite you to reflect on the insights gained and the transformations experienced. May this book serve as a guiding light on your path to prosperity, empowering you to unlock your full potential, achieve financial abundance, and live a life of purpose, fulfillment, and meaning. Remember that prosperity is not just about accumulating wealth for oneself, but about sharing abundance, creating positive change, and leaving a legacy that enriches the lives of others and inspires future generations.

As you continue your journey beyond these pages, may you embrace the principles of the prosperity paradigm and embody the values of integrity, resilience, and generosity. May you cultivate a mindset of abundance, gratitude, and possibility, and may you always strive to uplift and empower those around you. Together, let us envision a world where prosperity is not just a privilege for the few, but a reality for all, where financial freedom is attainable, and where each individual has the opportunity to thrive and flourish.